ASOKA AND ANCIENT INDIA

Alan Blackwood

Illustrated by Clyde Pearson

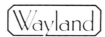

LIFE AND TIMES

Alexander the Great and the Greeks
Cleopatra and the Egyptians
Julius Caesar and the Romans
Alfred the Great and the Saxons
Canute and the Vikings
William the Conqueror and the Normans
Chaucer and the Middle Ages
Richard the Lionheart and the Crusades
Columbus and the Age of Exploration
Montezuma and the Aztecs
Elizabeth I and Tudor England
Atahuallpa and the Incas
Oliver Cromwell and the Civil War
Pepys and the Stuarts
Daniel Boone and the American West
Dickens and the Victorians
Boudicca and the Ancient Britons
Confucius and Ancient China
Sitting Bull and the Plains Indians
Nebuchadnezzer and the Babylonians
Asoka and Ancient India
Minos and the Cretans

Further titles are in preparation

First published in 1986 by
Wayland (Publishers) Ltd
61 Western Road, Hove
East Sussex BN3 1JD, England

© Copyright 1986 Wayland (Publishers) Ltd

British Library Cataloguing in Publication Data
Blackwood, Alan
Asoka and ancient India. — (Life and times)
1. India — History — to 324 B.C. — Juvenile literature
I. Title   II. Pearson, Clyde   III. Series
934   DS451

ISBN 0-85078-762-9

Phototypeset by Planagraphic Typesetters Ltd
Printed in Italy by G. Canale & C.S.p.A., Turin
Bound in the UK by The Bath Press, Avon

CONTENTS

1 ASOKA: EMPEROR AND MISSIONARY
Master of an empire 4
The edicts of stone 7
Asoka the missionary 8

2 INDIA'S ANCIENT HISTORY
The Indus Valley civilization 10
The Aryans 12
The end of an era 14

3 THE RELIGIONS OF INDIA
Hinduism 16
Buddhism and Jainism 18

4 AGRICULTURE, INDUSTRY AND TRADE
The farmer's life 20
Stone, clay and metal 22
India's ancient trade routes 24

5 GOVERNMENT AND LAW
Kings and ministers 26
The civil service 28

6 SCIENCE AND LEARNING
Astronomy 30
Mathematics 32
Medicine 34
Education 36

7 ARTS AND ENTERTAINMENTS
Architecture 38
Sculpture and painting 40
Music and dancing 42

Table of Dates 44
Glossary 45
Further information 46
Index 47

1 ASOKA: EMPEROR AND MISSIONARY

Master of an empire

Below Asoka's armies waged war on the people of Kalinga for many years.

The emblem or seal of modern India is a handsome group of lions. It was copied from the beautiful capital (top part) of a stone pillar which is over two thousand years old, and was made at the command of the Emperor Asoka, one of the greatest figures of India's long and wonderful past.

Asoka, or Asokavardhana to give him his full name, lived from about 300BC to 232BC. For over forty years he ruled the Mauryan empire. With its capital city at Pataliputra (near Patna, by the river Ganges), this mighty empire of over 100 million people extended from the Bay of Bengal in the east to the snowy mountains of Tibet, Persia (Iran) and Afghanistan in the north and west, and the baking hot Deccan plateau in the south.

4

One of Asoka's first acts, after he came to the throne in 273BC, was to enlarge his domains still further. In about the year 265BC he led his armies in a war of conquest against the neighbouring state of Kalinga, on India's eastern coast. The people of Kalinga stubbornly resisted Asoka's invasion, and the war dragged on for several years. Tens of thousands of people died in battle; thousands more perished from hunger and disease.

Asoka won in the end, but he did not celebrate his victory with parades. By this time, he was appalled at the misery and horror of war, and swore never to take up arms again. He had found a far better and more enlightened way to rule.

Above   Throughout the centuries the teachings of Buddhism have
continued to influence people in the paths of peace and respect for
all life, in the same way that they influenced Asoka over two
thousand years ago.

The edicts of stone

Asoka was brought up as a Hindu, the ancient religion of India. It was, however, the teachings of Buddhism which did most to change him from a man of war to a man of peace. Buddhism taught that greed, bloodshed and violence could never make people happy. The only way to find peace of mind, said Buddhists, was through honest work, truthfulness, kindness and respect for the lives of all creatures, human and otherwise.

Asoka was so impressed by such attitudes and ideas that he wanted everyone else to know about them. So, throughout the length and breadth of his empire, he had edicts or messages inscribed in stone — the best way to spread information in the days before there was proper paper to write on.

Here are the opening words of one of them: 'Thus saith His Majesty. Father and mother must be obeyed; similarly respect for living creatures must be enforced; truth must be spoken. These are the virtues of the Law of Duty which must be practised.' Another edict warns people against such feelings as 'envy, harshness, impatience and laziness.' The way the edicts are written gives the impression that Asoka himself was a stern, but just and humane man.

Some of his inscriptions were made on large rocks and boulders, some were cut onto the rock walls of caves. The finest appeared on specially-built stone columns or pillars, such as the one at Sarnath, near the holy city of Varanasi, formerly Benares, crowned with the famous lions and the Wheel of Law or Authority.

Above *One of Asoka's edicts informing his people of how they should live their lives.*

Asoka the missionary

The Emperor Asoka was so keen to spread the knowledge of Buddhism that he sent missionary expeditions beyond the frontiers of his own empire. Some historians believe he may have dispatched missionaries as far afield as Africa and to such Mediterranean lands as Turkey and Greece. The expeditions we know about are those he sent to Tibet, south India, Burma and Sri Lanka (Ceylon).

Asoka's mission to the lovely tropical island of Sri Lanka, lying off the southern tip of India, was the most successful of all. It was led by Prince Mahendra (sometimes called Mahinda), who was probably Asoka's youngest brother. He was welcomed by the island's King Tissa, and together they converted almost everybody to

Below *The massive statue of a reclining Buddha at Polonnaruwa in Sri Lanka.*

the Buddhist faith. They also created some of the most spectacular of all Buddhist monuments. At Anuradhapura, for example, they built great, dome-shaped temples or stupas. Another world-famous Buddhist shrine in Sri Lanka is at Polonnaruwa, where there are beautiful rock carvings, including one of a huge reclining, or resting, Buddha.

Asoka died in or about the year 232BC. Control of the Mauryan empire passed to his sons and grandsons. Little is known about them, but the empire itself did not survive for long after the end of Asoka's strong but kindly rule. A mere fifty years after his death, it had broken up.

He had, however, left behind him, in his rock and pillar inscriptions, the greatest record of ancient Indian civilization. And he had established Buddhism as one of the world's great religions.

2 INDIA'S ANCIENT HISTORY

The Indus Valley civilization

Although the Emperor Asoka lived so long ago, the history of the Indian sub-continent (including what is now India itself, Pakistan and Bangladesh) is far older still. Two thousand years before Asoka was born, there existed the Indus Valley civilization, named after the River Indus which flows down the length of present-day Pakistan, from the Himalayan mountains to the Arabian Sea.

The Indus Valley civilization dates from about 2500BC, which makes it as old as the civilizations of Egypt, China, and Sumer (Babylonia) in the Middle East. It was as remarkable as any of them.

One of its cities was at Mohenjodaro, right by the Indus, where archaeologists have unearthed a foundation of broad streets, crossing each other at regular intervals, much like the streets of New York and other modern cities. Houses were solidly built of bricks, and stone conduits indicate a good water supply and drainage system. On the same site they found many earthenware and metal artefacts — bowls, dishes, cups, spoons, pots and pans — and impressive figures sculpted from stone or fashioned from bronze, copper and silver.

At both Mohenjodaro and Harappa, about 550km (350 miles) further up the Indus Valley, archaeologists have also discovered the foundations of citadels or fortified palaces, and of granaries for storing rice or other grain crops.

There is much about the Indus Valley civilization which remains a mystery after all this time; but from what we have already discovered, we know that its people were highly skilled craftsmen, engineers and builders, and that their society was very well ordered and administered.

Above *A terracotta figure found at the site of the ancient city of Mohenjodaro.*

Right *Mohenjodaro was a city of broad streets and solidly built houses, with a good water supply and efficient drainage system.*

11

ARYAN HOMELANDS

Aral
Sea

Caspian
Sea

HINDU KUSH

Harappa

HIMALAYAS

R. Indus

Mohenjodaro

R. Ganges

Arabian Sea

SRI LANKA

12

The Aryans

The Aryans were one of the most important races of people in world history, because of their influence on other societies and cultures. Their original homeland was somewhere in southern Russia or the Middle East. Then about 1500BC they began to spread out in different directions. Some moved westwards into Europe, others moved south and east into the Indian sub-continent. As a result, they formed a strong link between the peoples of Europe and of Asia, so that we can speak of an entire Indo-Aryan or Indo-European race and culture.

Those Aryans who moved into what is today India, Bangladesh and Pakistan had a tremendous effect on the region. They first attacked and destroyed the Indus Valley civilization, forcing many of the Indus Valley folk (Dravidians) to migrate to southern India, where they now form such present-day racial groups as the Tamils. Elsewhere, the relatively fair-skinned Aryans gradually intermingled with the darker-skinned native populations and settled down.

Among their many achievements, these Indo-Aryans produced the language and script of Sanskrit, from which has come Hindi, the official language of modern India. They also created a marvellous literature, based on the hymns and other sacred poems to their gods. In course of time, these were written down in Sanskrit, and were called the Vedas. The Aryan civilization is called the Vedic period.

As we shall see, the Vedas became the foundation of the Hindu faith, which, in turn, has affected most aspects of Indian life and thought for over two thousand years.

Left *The map shows the migration routes of the Aryan peoples into the Indian sub-continent.*

13

The end of an era

Above *The Muslims spread the religion of Islam through North Africa, Spain, the Middle East and into India.*

Throughout India's immensely long history, the pendulum has swung between very good and very bad times.

After Asoka, there were other kings and emperors who brought peace and prosperity to the land. One group, who ruled from about AD320 to 480, are known as the Gupta dynasty. The arts and sciences reached a peak of beauty and wisdom at that time. Another time of enlightenment and advance was the reign of King Harsha, who ruled most of India from AD608 to 647. 'In all the highways of the towns and villages,' one chronicler wrote, 'he built hostels, provided food and drink, and physicians (doctors) for travellers and the poor people.'

There were also, by contrast, periods of bloodshed, famine and ruin. In about AD500 a race of wild horsemen from central Asia, the Huns, rode across Kashmir and the Punjab and on into the heart of India, plundering, killing, and destroying the good work of the Gupta kings. The Rajputs, or 'Sons of Kings', who followed King Harsha, brought more centuries of misery as they quarrelled and fought amongst themselves.

Then, about the year 1000, came the Muslims. They were followers of the religion of Islam, who had already conquered most of North Africa and Spain, and the whole of the Middle East. Among the Muslim leaders to invade India was the Sultan Muhmad. In 1024 he fought his way into one of India's most sacred Hindu shrines, at Somnath by the Arabian Sea, and with one mighty blow from his sword he shattered the statue to the god Shiva. It was the end of one era of Indian history, and the beginning of another.

Right *Sultan Muhmad and his armies fought their way into one of India's most sacred Hindu shrines, where the statue of the god Shiva was shattered.*

3 THE RELIGIONS OF INDIA

Hinduism

Above *A tenth-century stone carving of the god Vishnu as the supreme cosmic prince, with Brahma and Shiva on either side.*

Below *The Hindu gods (left to right) Brahma, Vishnu, Shiva.*

Hinduism is the oldest world religion still practised by millions of people. Unlike other major religions, it was not founded by a particular prophet or teacher, but developed over many centuries. Some of its beliefs go right back to the time of the Indus Valley civilization; but the Vedas, the hymns composed by the Aryan people, form the basis of Hinduism as we know it.

There are hundreds of gods and goddesses in Hinduism, some represented as human beings, others as birds, monkeys and other creatures. Four of the best known are Brahma, the creator of life, Vishnu, the preserver, Shiva the destroyer, and the elephant-headed Ganesa, protector of the home and family. Yet the Vedas and other scriptures say that all these gods are really only different aspects of the one supreme god, or universal spirit, called Brahman. So we can think of the Hindu religion as being either polytheistic (with many gods) or

monotheistic (with one god, like Christianity, Judaism or Islam).

Hindus also believe in reincarnation. This is the belief that our souls progress through many physical lives, until they are spiritually pure enough to be united with the power or spirit of Brahman. Then we leave earthly existence behind.

To help them achieve this spiritual goal, Indian holy men have, for thousands of years, practised forms of yoga. Yoga means 'yoke' or 'union', and the aim of yoga exercises is to concentrate the powers of body and mind so that the soul, too, gains in strength.

Buddhism and Jainism

Hinduism has given rise to other religions. The greatest of these is Buddhism. Its founder was Prince Siddhartha Gautama, known as the Buddha (Enlightened One), who lived in north India about three hundred years before Asoka. As well as teaching kindness and toleration, the Buddha said that the cause of suffering was the desire for unattainable things. A person who could eliminate desire from his or her way of life might reach spiritual peace and perfection *(nirvana)* and so bring to an end the process of birth and re-birth. To do this, the person must give up all worldly ambition, calm the body and mind and live only for others.

Another religious teacher who lived in India at about the same time as the Buddha was Vardhamana Mahavira, called Jina (which means Victorious). He, too, spoke of desire as the prime cause of suffering, and recommended a life of asceticism — denying the body all normal pleasures and comforts — as the way to shake off desire and attain *nirvana*. His followers, called Jains, also believe that all life, plant and animal, has its own soul and is therefore sacred. Jains will not kill any animal for food, and may even ask others to cook their vegetables for them, rather than harm the plants themselves. Such a belief is called *ahimsa*.

It is interesting to compare the history of these two religions. Buddhism has never been a major religion in India itself but, thanks to Asoka, it spread to many other countries of the East — Sri Lanka, Burma, Thailand, China and Japan. Jainism, by contrast, has had a strong influence in India, but has never been widely taken up by other nations.

Left *Sweeping the pathway in front of oxen so that no insects will be trodden on — in the Jain tradition of preserving all life.*

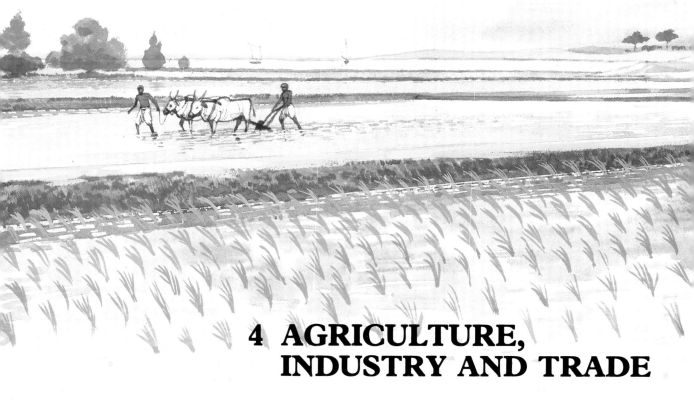

4 AGRICULTURE, INDUSTRY AND TRADE

The farmer's life

Indian history began in the Neolithic Age (or New Stone Age) — about 7,000 years ago — when men and women first settled in village communities and started to grow crops, instead of wandering from place to place in search of food. By the time of the Indus Valley civilization, such farming was already a well-organized way of life, as we know from the evidence of the granaries and storage pits found at Mohenjodaro, Harappa and elsewhere. The farmers tilled the fields with wooden ploughs and irrigated them during the blazing hot summer months.

The pattern for Indian farming and agriculture was even more firmly established after the Aryan invasion. Most people lived in villages, each farmer working a small plot of land for himself and his family. He probably kept a cow for milk, and one or two bullocks for drawing the plough or raising leather buckets of water from rivers or wells. But being Hindus, most farmers were vegetarians,

and did not raise cattle for meat. Besides, cattle need pasture, which most farmers did not possess.

The principal crop was rice, which had to be grown in the low-lying marshy ground of river deltas, or in specially flooded fields called paddies. In his homeland in the Ganges river valley, Asoka must have looked upon the watery stretches of the paddy fields, and seen the farmers bending to their task of planting out the young green rice plants. No doubt he joined them in prayers to the gods for a good crop. For if anything went wrong — if, for example, the monsoon rains should fail — and the rice did not grow, then millions of his subjects would starve.

Cotton, too, has played a vital role in the life of the Indian people. The fleecy fibres of the cotton plant's seed-head are spun into long threads of yarn and then woven on a loom to make cotton fabrics. This is a craft which was already old when the Emperor Asoka was born; it is still carried on, with little change, in India today. Although there are many fine, brightly coloured cotton fabrics to be found, the basic white cotton dhoti (a type of loincloth), turban and sari have clothed the Indian people for over four thousand years.

21

Stone, clay and metal

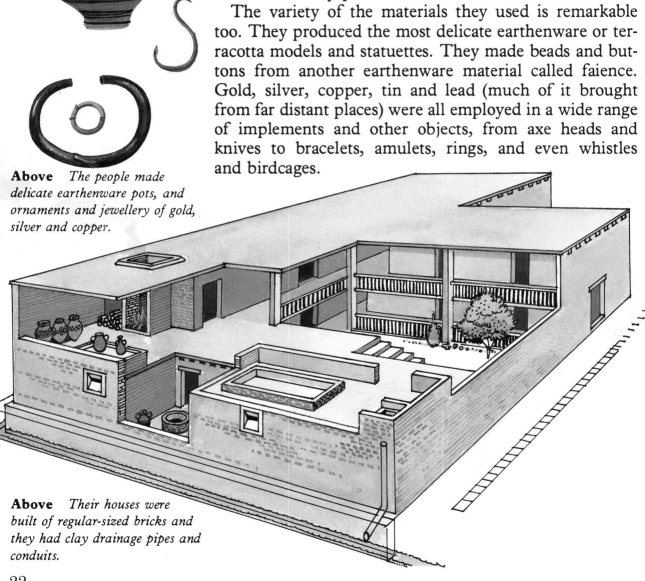

The Indus Valley people were leaders in what we might call the 'high technology' of the ancient world. They made clay pipes for drains and water conduits, when people elsewhere still used only stone. Their mud bricks were made to a perfectly regular size and weight. They were probably the inventors of the potter's wheel, to turn and fashion clay pots and bowls.

The variety of the materials they used is remarkable too. They produced the most delicate earthenware or terracotta models and statuettes. They made beads and buttons from another earthenware material called faience. Gold, silver, copper, tin and lead (much of it brought from far distant places) were all employed in a wide range of implements and other objects, from axe heads and knives to bracelets, amulets, rings, and even whistles and birdcages.

Above *The people made delicate earthenware pots, and ornaments and jewellery of gold, silver and copper.*

Above *Their houses were built of regular-sized bricks and they had clay drainage pipes and conduits.*

Above *Indian craftsmen became the most skilled iron workers in the world.*

Below *The Iron Pillar of Delhi, made in about AD 300.*

By 1000BC, Indian craftsmen were probably beginning to experiment with the smelting (extracting from its ore), casting and forging of iron. In the centuries that followed, they became the most skilled iron workers in the world, even learning how to convert iron into steel. The Iron Pillar of Delhi (dating from about AD300) shows just how good they were. This masterpiece of metalwork is over 7 m (22 ft) high, weighs over 6 tonnes, and is made from sections of wrought (forged) iron hammered together. After more than 1,500 years of exposure to tropical sun and monsoon rains, it shows no sign of rust or any other corrosion.

Yet another ancient Indian skill was the polishing or burnishing of stone. By methods now lost to us, they could make the surface of certain kinds of rock as smooth and clear as the finest mirror.

India's ancient trade routes

When the Portuguese explorer Vasco da Gama first sailed to India and back in the closing years of the fifteenth century, people in Europe thought he had discovered a new and mysterious land. In fact, India was doing a brisk trade with many other parts of the world long before the nations of modern Europe existed.

One of India's trade routes, first used by the Indus Valley people, was overland, north-westwards through the famous Kyber Pass, to link up with the 'silk highway' that stretched right across central Asia from the Mediterranean Sea to China.

The Phoenicians of the eastern Mediterranean, who were among the greatest seafarers of the ancient world, sailed to and from India, down the Red Sea and across the Arabian Sea, bringing back cargoes of ivory, gemstones, fine-woven cloth and other profitable merchandise.

Alexander the Great's invasion of the Indian subcontinent in the 4th century BC opened up a new and flourishing trade between India and the Greek city-states, where Indian metalware was highly valued. Many Greek coins found in India testify how important that trade became.

During and after Asoka's time, the Romans were equally keen to buy India's products, from metalware and fabrics, to pepper and other rare spices. Alexandria, by the mouth of the River Nile, was a great transit port for all this trade between India, Greece and Rome.

Ancient India traded with China too. The spread of Buddhism, started by Asoka, was important in establishing this. Buddhist missionaries reached China about AD65, and soon Indian merchants were exporting iron and steel and buying Chinese silk in return.

Below *A camel caravan carrying goods through the Khyber Pass to link up with the silk highway that stretched right across Asia.*

5 GOVERNMENT AND LAW

Kings and ministers

Above *The base of a column showing part of one of Asoka's many edicts.*

Right *At his coronation a new king would bow low before his ministers to show his respect for them — the Indus Valley kings had to consult their ministers on all matters.*

King Chandragupta Maurya, Asoka's grandfather, was a powerful and ruthless man whose word was law. Asoka himself was also a strong and influential leader. Nevertheless, the rulers of India on the whole did not wield nearly as much power in their lands as did the pharaohs of Egypt, or other kings and emperors of the ancient world.

From early times, wise men in India warned against rulers with too much power, or kings who thought they should be treated like gods. 'Sovereignty is possible only with assistance,' stated one famous text on law and government. 'A single wheel can never move. Hence the king shall employ ministers and hear their opinion.' At his coronation, a new king had to bow low before his ministers — usually Brahmins (people of the highest caste or class) — and from then on he was expected to consult them on all matters of state. If he failed to do this, they might well depose him, or even have him killed.

Asoka, in his edicts, spoke often of his subjects as his 'children', meaning that it was his solemn duty to look after them. He was indeed a model of Indian kingship — always prepared to listen to people's complaints, to act as judge in disputes between them, to gather taxes and spend the money wisely on public works.

Some of the states of ancient India did not have kings at all. They were among the world's first republics, governed by an assembly which reached its decisions through debate and a free vote. We often think of the ancient Greeks as pioneers of the democratic way of life; but they may well have received their political ideas from the even older governments of India.

Above *A scene at a river crossing on the Great Royal Highway. Tax collectors are inspecting goods entering their province.*

The civil service

India's kings and emperors — good or bad — were only a small part of the government. For long periods of history, the running of the country was largely in the hands of a civil service. During the time of the Mauryan empire (from Chandragupta to his grandson Asoka) this reached a peak of efficiency. The empire was divided into provinces, each with its own governor and team of officials. Individual towns and cities were similarly divided. Within them were boards or departments, each with their own special duty. One department collected taxes on land or

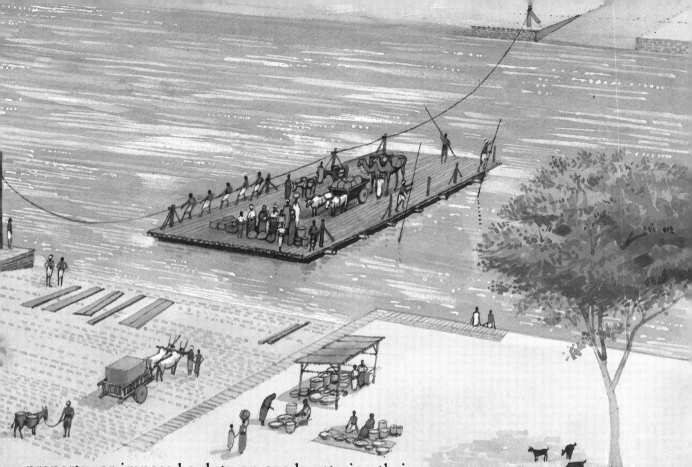

property, or imposed a duty on goods entering their province (a kind of customs and excise office). Other departments carried out a regular census of births and deaths, supervised the fair use of weights and measures, or checked on standards of manufacture and craftsmanship.

Schools, universities and hospitals were built using public funds, so creating a kind of welfare state. One of the most impressive of all public works in the Mauryan empire was the Great Royal Highway. This linked the city of Taxila in the north-west of the empire with the capital of Pataliputra, continuing on to the Bay of Bengal — a distance of over 2,500 km (1,600 miles). It was provided with signposts, roadside trees for shade, and bridges and ferries at each river or stream along the route. The Romans, whom we think of as the master builders and engineers of the ancient world, never built a greater road than the Great Royal Highway.

29

6 SCIENCE AND LEARNING

Astronomy

Indian wise men and scholars, like people nearly everywhere, were fascinated by the wonders of the heavens. They practised astrology — trying to see into the future by interpreting the positions of the sun, moon and stars in the sky. At the same time they were pioneers in astronomy — the true scientific study of the heavens. Without telescopes to help them, they listed hundreds of stars or constellations (star groups), and accurately plotted the passage of the sun across the sky through twelve sections or months of the year, so providing the basis for our modern calendar.

Most remarkable of all, perhaps, were the conclusions reached by these scholars. They reasoned, quite correctly, that although the sun appears to move across the sky, it is really the Earth that is moving and not the sun. They were also quite right when they said that the moon has no light of its own, but shines with the reflected light of the sun.

Greatest of all Indian astronomers was Aryabhata, who was born about AD470. He described the Earth as a sphere, rotating on its own axis and revolving round the sun, so explaining the sequence of day and night and the seasons of the year. He also put forward ideas about the solar system — of the Earth being only one of a number of planets going round the sun. Moreover, he believed that the attraction of the planets towards each other (gravity) held them in position.

Although Aryabhata lived a thousand years before the famous European astronomers Copernicus, Galileo and Sir Isaac Newton, he had already noted many of the discoveries they were later to make.

Left *Indian scholars studied astronomy. Without the use of telescopes, they listed many of the constellations and plotted the passage of the sun.*

31

Above *The ancient Indians were skilled mathematicians and were able to calculate complex geometrical proportions.*

Mathematics

Aryabhata, like many astronomers, was also a great mathematician — another science at which the learned men of ancient India excelled.

Geometry was probably the first branch of mathematics they explored. Temples and other holy shrines were built to special dimensions, which meant they had to calculate lengths and angles and volumes — just as the ancient

Left *Their knowledge of mathematics enabled the Indians to build temples and other holy buildings to carefully calculated dimensions. This is the entrance to a Royal Pavilion on Sri Lanka, built in the eleventh and twelfth centuries.*

Egyptians worked out the angles and proportions of the pyramids. Indian mathematicians also studied the diameter and circumference of a circle, and the even more complex geometry of cones and spheres. It is likely that Euclid, Pythagoras and other famous Greek thinkers of a later date received much of their knowledge from India.

The greatest breakthrough made by Indian mathematicians was to express the idea of nothingness — that is, they made use of a term or symbol to represent zero value. This was a real revolution in arithmetic, because it made their methods of calculation more flexible, and allowed them to deal in far higher values than had been possible when every number from one upwards had its own special sign. Our own decimal system of addition, subtraction, multiplication and division, using numbers in sets of tens, hundreds and thousands, owes a great deal to the Indian mathematicians of ancient times.

Indian scholars also used the value of zero to create a form of algebra, at the same time using letters to represent unknown values which could then be revealed by measuring them, or relating them to known values. Many people believe that the Arabs invented both decimal arithmetic and algebra. But the Arabs themselves learnt these skills from the Indians.

Medicine

When Alexander the Great invaded north-west India in 326BC, he was amazed to find doctors in the opposing armies who could cure snake bites and carry out surgery on the wounded. No other armies he had met provided such medical care, and he was quick to recruit Indian doctors and surgeons to his own ranks.

The Indus Valley people already had a good understanding of medical hygiene, to judge by the care they took at Mohenjodaro over drains, water supply and sanitation. By Asoka's time, the science of medicine had advanced so far that there were hospitals for the treatment of disease and injury.

Some doctors were expert in the use of herbs and in drugs extracted from plants to cure disease, deal with cases of poisoning or to administer as painkillers and sedatives. One of their texts lists 750 species of plant with

Below *Indian surgeons were expert at setting bones and treating other injuries.*

medicinal properties. Other doctors studied anatomy, and had a basic understanding of the circulation of the blood and the working of the nervous system. Surgeons were expert at setting broken bones and treating injuries to the face (a kind of plastic surgery), using scalpels and other instruments quite like modern ones. They also used fumigation (wood smoke) as a way of sterilizing instruments and wounds.

As well as treatment of the sick, there was, in ancient India, plenty of medical advice on how to stay fit. Doctors recommended regular sleep and regular meals, and taught people how to clean their teeth. One ancient Indian practice which is fast coming back into favour today is massage with various oils, to tone up the skin and relax both body and mind.

Above *Their doctors were skilled in the use of herbs and drugs.*

Right *When Alexander the Great invaded India he found a people whose knowledge of medicine greatly surpassed that of his own surgeons.*

Above *A student learns spiritual enlightenment from a guru.*

Education

Religion and education went hand in hand in ancient India. The Vedas and other Hindu scriptures did not set out a system of beliefs for people simply to adopt. Instead they were full of philosophical ideas which readers had to think out for themselves. This introduced people to education and knowledge in a broader sense. Education, for them, was a way of reaching spiritual enlightenment.

Education often started with instruction from a guru or wise man. He did not cram his students' heads full of facts and figures, but taught them to regard education as a way of learning about themselves, a path to self-awareness and wisdom. He would also send them off on errands, or to beg for food, to teach them obedience and humility.

Those wishing to study the scriptures, or one of the arts or sciences, went to a university. For many centuries, these were paid for out of public funds, and were open to all, men and women, rich and poor alike, provided they were clever enough. Students joined in debates, which trained them to think deeply and express themselves clearly, and were instructed in their chosen subjects. Finally, they were closely examined by their own teachers, who decided when they were properly qualified.

After the time of Asoka and the spread of Buddhism, many Buddhist monasteries also became seats of learning. Most famous of these was at Nalanda, not far from Asoka's own capital city of Pataliputra. Students from many other lands — such as Sri Lanka, Burma, China — all wanted to go to Nalanda, which had a great library of scrolls and inscriptions. No wonder India, for so many centuries, was ahead of every other country in the fields of astronomy, mathematics, medicine, and much else besides.

Below *Students from many lands came to the monastery at Nalanda.*

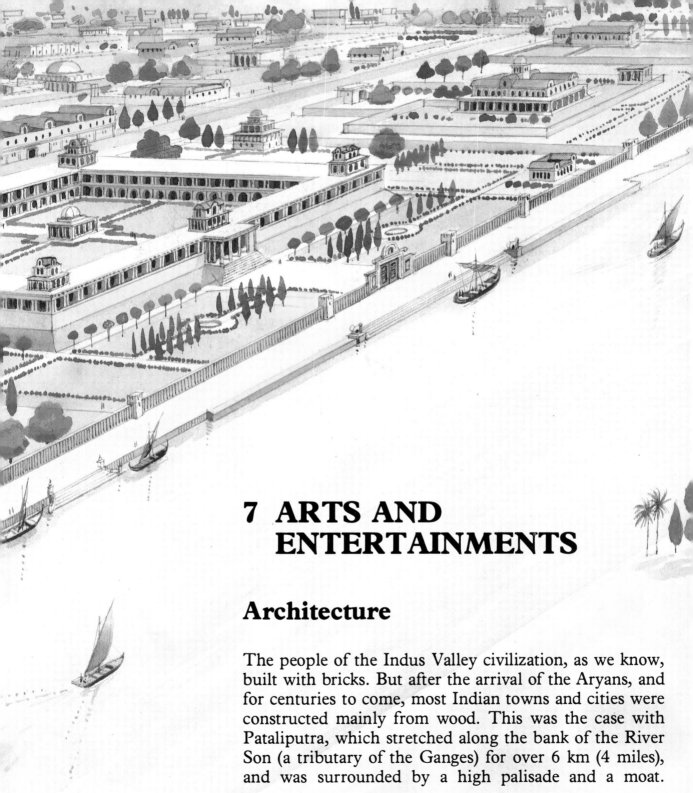

7 ARTS AND ENTERTAINMENTS

Architecture

The people of the Indus Valley civilization, as we know, built with bricks. But after the arrival of the Aryans, and for centuries to come, most Indian towns and cities were constructed mainly from wood. This was the case with Pataliputra, which stretched along the bank of the River Son (a tributary of the Ganges) for over 6 km (4 miles), and was surrounded by a high palisade and a moat.

Asoka's imperial palace, standing in beautiful gardens, had wooden columns and beams decorated with carved images of plants and animals and painted in gilt.

Bricks and stone were reserved for religious monuments. One of these was the stupa, a type of shrine to the gods, with a dome-like structure. After Asoka's conversion to Buddhism, he built several stupas containing relics of the Buddha. One of the most famous of these is at Sanchi (near the modern city of Bhopal), enclosed by a high stone wall with four massive gateways. Even greater stupas were built in other countries where Buddhism had spread, such as the one at Anuradhapura in Sri Lanka, which was as high as London's St Paul's Cathedral.

At the time of the Gupta dynasty (AD320 to 480), magnificent temples were built. They were usually planned round a courtyard, with several shrine rooms and a main hall for worshippers. They had flat roofs, supported by thick stone columns and were surmounted by large brick or stone towers. In north India, the towers have curved sides and a rounded top. Further south, they look more like steep-sided pyramids with the top cut off, and are elaborately carved and painted with the images of gods.

Left *Asoka's capital city of Pataliputra stretched along the bank of the River Son.*

Below and right *The Stupa at Sanchi, which is enclosed by a high wall with large gateways, and a temple in southern India of the Gupta dynasty.*

Below *The beautifully sculpted head of a bearded man found at Mohenjodaro.*

Sculpture and painting

The Indus Valley people were highly skilled in the plastic arts — modelling in clay, metals and other materials; also the carving of rock and stone. Their beautifully fashioned clay and bronze figurines are works of art; and one, the stone head and shoulders of a bearded man found at Mohenjodaro, is a 4,000-year-old sculptural masterpiece.

From the start of the Vedic (Aryan) period, Indian artists were inspired by the images of the various gods and goddesses. They produced countless gold and bronze statues of the god Shiva performing his 'cosmic' dance; and they filled every inch of temple walls and columns with god-like figures, lying, sitting and dancing so that whole buildings seem to burst with life and movement.

The most breathtaking achievements of India's stone-masons and sculptors are temples and shrines actually cut into hills and cliffs. At Ajanta, about 350km (220 miles) from Bombay, twenty-seven cave temples were excavated, some of them penetrating 30 m (nearly 100 ft) into the rock, decorated with both sculpture and vivid paintings of gods and animals. At nearby Ellora, a succession of artists toiled for centuries to turn one entire rock face into an open-air temple, with halls, cloisters and columns.

Above all, there is Asoka's Lion Pillar at Sarnath, the finest monument we have, both to Asoka himself and to the work of Indian artists.

Above *Asoka's Lion Pillar at Sarnath.*

Below *The wonderfully carved shrine at Ellora.*

Above *A group of Indian musicians playing traditional sitars and drums.*

Music and dancing

The ancient Indians believed music was a magical gift from the gods; something powerful enough to conjure up fire or storms. They also believed there was a proper place and time for the performance of each piece of music, and to play it at the wrong time might harm the souls of players and listeners alike.

Most traditional Indian music is played on a stringed instrument such as the sitar, with accompanying drums, and is based on what are called *ragas*. Each *raga* is a fairly short melody, or sequence of notes, which the player repeats many times over, changing it slightly each time as the inspiration of the moment takes him. The drummers can also make very subtle changes in the rhythm. Another feature of a *raga* is that it usually begins quite slowly and gradually speeds up, creating an almost hypnotic effect on listeners.

Just as the slightest change of melody or rhythm is of great importance in music, so each tiny gesture means something special in Indian dancing. Ancient texts on the subject list hundreds of poses, involving feet, hands, positions of the neck and head, even movement of the eyes — positions of the body which we can see represented in many of those stone carvings and statues of the gods. Indian dancers practise for years and have perfect control over every muscle of their bodies.

Today, traditional Indian music and dancing is popular in Western countries such as Britain and the United States of America. Listening to a *raga*, or watching the graceful and subtle movements of Indian dancers, is a pleasure in itself. Their music and dances can also remind us of the Emperor Asoka and of a remarkable civilization to which we owe so much; in the fields of mathematics, medicine and astronomy, in the arts and crafts, and in philosophy, religion and good government.

Below *Indian dancers practice for years to perfect the hundreds of different movements, each of which has a special meaning.*

43

Table of Dates

c.3000 -1500BC	Indus Valley civilization.
c.1500BC	Aryan invasion of India.
c.1000BC	Writing of the Vedas and foundation of Hinduism.
c.560BC	Birth of Siddhartha Gautama, the Buddha.
326BC	Alexander the Great invades India.
c.320BC	Chandragupta Maurya founds the Mauryan empire.
273- 232BC	Reign of Emperor Asoka and spread of Buddhism.
AD**320 -480**	Gupta dynasty and a golden age of Indian arts and sciences.
AD**500**	Hun invasion of India.
AD**608 -647**	Reign of King Harsha and a new period of peace and prosperity.
c.AD**1000**	Muslim invasion and end of ancient Indian history.

'c' ('circa' in Latin) before a date means that the exact date is not known.

Picture acknowledgements

Bill Donohoe 16 (artwork); Hutchison Library 23; Mansell Collection 10, 26; Outlook Films 6; Ronald Sheridan's Photo Library 7, 16 (top), 33, 34, 41 (top and bottom); Wayland Picture Library 14.

Glossary

Ahimsa Sanskrit for 'no injury'; the doctrine that all life is sacred and should not be harmed.

Archaeology Study of prehistory; i.e. history before people kept a written record of events.

Aryan Peoples whose ancestry originated in central Asia, and who moved into the Indian sub-continent in about 1500BC, also linking up with European peoples.

Asceticism Leading a life of self-denial, without normal pleasures or comforts.

Bronze Dark metal alloy (mixture), mainly of copper and tin.

Burnish To polish by hard rubbing.

Census Record of population (e.g. register of births and deaths).

Chronicle Diary or record of events; hence 'chronicler', one who keeps such a record.

Dhoti Type of loincloth for men (i.e. worn around the waist).

Dynasty Succession of rulers of the same family line.

Earthenware Items made from baked clay; pottery.

Edict A decree or command.

Faience Type of decorated earthenware.

Forge To heat iron or other metals until they are soft enough to hammer into different shapes.

Gilt Thin layer of gold; hence 'gilded', covered with gold.

Guru A religious teacher.

Irrigate To supply land with water from reservoirs, dams, channels and pipes.

Missionary Person who tries to convert others to his or her religious beliefs.

Monsoon Asian name for certain winds, especially those that bring heavy seasonal rains.

Nirvana Sanskrit for 'extinguish'; spiritual enlightenment in Hinduism and Buddhism.

Palisade High defensive wooden fence.

Raga Sanskrit for 'musical tone'; principal type of traditional Indian music, based on a particular sequence of notes.

Reincarnation 'Return in the flesh'; Hindu belief that a person's soul has many bodily lives.

Sanskrit Ancient sacred and scholarly language and writing of India.

Sari Length of cotton or silk draped round the body, worn by Indian women.

Scroll Roll of parchment or paper, usually with text written upon it.

Shrine Place of worship.

Sitar Indian stringed musical instrument.

Smelt To extract metal from an ore by heating.

Stupa Circular, dome-like building, mostly a type of Buddhist shrine.

Terracotta 'Baked earth'; a reddish type of earthenware.

Turban Type of scarf wound round the head.

Vedas Sanskrit for 'sacred knowledge'; sacred scriptures, the basis of Hinduism.

Yoga Sanskrit for 'yoke' or 'union'; exercises of mind or body to help the soul reach spiritual perfection (*nirvana*).

Further information

Books
There are not many books on ancient Indian history, but here are some that are very interesting to study.

Ancient Civilizations, Anne Millard (Kingfisher, 1982).
Asoka, R. K. Mookergee (Orient Book distributors 1972).
Indian Art, Roy C. Craven (Thames and Hudson, 1976). This book includes many splendid illustrations of the temples and other places and art objects described in this book.
Life World Library: India, Joe David Brown (Time-Life International, 1967). This is a fairly old publication, but many of its colourful pictures give a very good idea of traditional Indian life and culture.
The First Civilizations, Alan Millard. History in Pictures series (Macmillan 1979).

Places to visit
If you are able to travel to India, try to visit the caves at Ajanta and Ellora, about 400 km (250 miles) inland from Bombay. You can see the stone pillar and stupas at Sarnath, just north of Varanasi (formerly Benares) and the Iron Pillar at Delhi. The site of the ancient city of Mohenjodaro is in Pakistan, on the River Indus, about 160 km (100 miles) north of Hyderabad. In Sri Lanka, you should see the stupas at Anuradhapura and the wonderful rock carvings at Polonnaruwa.

If you are in London, the Victoria and Albert Museum in South Kensington has many beautiful pieces of ancient Indian sculpture and metalwork, very like those described in this book.

Index

Agriculture 20-21
Ajanta, cave temples at 41
Alexander the Great 25, 34
Aryabhata 31, 32
Architecture 32, 38-9
Art 40-41
Aryan people, invasion
by 13, 20
  effects on Indus Valley
    people 13
Asoka, Emperor 4-5, 7, 8,
  20-21, 26
  character 5, 7
  edicts 7
  religion 7, 8-9
  rule 5, 7, 9, 26, 28-9

Buddha 8-9, 18
Buddhism 7, 8-9, 18, 24, 39
Buddhist missionaries 8, 25, 37
Buddhist monasteries 37
Building 22, 32, 39

Chandragupta Maurya, King
  26, 28
Civil service 28
Cotton weaving 21
Crafts 10, 22-3, 40-41, 43

Dancing 42-3
Drainage systems 10, 22, 34

Education 36-7
Ellora, cave shrine at 41

Gods
  Brahma 16
  Ganesa 16, 17
  Shiva 14, 16, 40
  Vishnu 16
Government 26, 43
Gupta dynasty 14, 39
Guru 36-7

Harappa 20
Harsha, King 14
Hindi 13
Hindu shrines 14
Hinduism 13, 16-17
Hospitals 34
Huns 14

Iron Pillar of Delhi 23, 41
Iron smelting 23
Islam 14, 17

Jainism 18
Jain temple 18

Khyber Pass 24, 25

Mahendra, Prince 8
Mathematics 32-3, 43
Mauryan empire 4, 9, 28-9
Medical skills 34-5, 43
Metal working 23
Mohenjodaro 10, 35, 40
Music 42-3
Muslims 14

Nalanda 37

Painting 40
Pataliputra 4, 29, 37
Philosophy 43
Pottery 10, 22

Rajputs 14
Reincarnation 17
River Indus 10

Sanitation 34
Sanskrit 13
Scholars 31, 32-3
Sculpture 40
Silk highway 24, 25
Sri Lanka 8, 18, 37
Stone pillars 4, 7, 41
Students 36-7
Stupas 9, 39
Sultan Muhmad 14

Temples 7, 8, 33, 39, 41
Trade routes 24-5

Vedas 13, 16, 36
Vedic period 13

Water channels 10, 22